Katharine Drexel

Blessed Are the Meek

1858–1955

Born in Philadelphia, Pennsylvania

Feast Day: March 3

Patron of racial justice and philanthropists

"Blessed are the meek, for they shall inherit the land."
Matthew 5:5

Text by Barbara Yoffie
Illustrated by Chris Sharp

Liguori Publications
A Redemptorist Ministry

Dedication

To my family:
my parents Jim and Peg,
my husband Bill,
our son Sam and daughter-in-law Erin,
and our precious grandchildren
Ben, Lucas, and Andrew

To all the children I have had the privilege
of teaching throughout the years.

Imprimi Potest:
Kevin Zubel, CSsR, Provincial
Denver Province, the Redemptorists

Published by Liguori Publications, Liguori, Missouri 63057
To order, visit Liguori.org or call 800-325-9521.

ISBN (print): 978-0-7648-2865-2
ISBN (digital): 978-0-7648-7248-8

Liguori Publications, a nonprofit corporation, is an apostolate of the Redemptorists. To learn more about the Redemptorists, visit Redemptorists.com.

Printed in the United States of America
27 26 25 24 23 / 5 4 3 2 1
First Edition

Dear Parents and Teachers:

Saints and Me! is a six-set series of children's books about saints, including the: *Saints of North America* who served our homeland; *Saints of Christmas*, who teach us to love Jesus; *Saints for Families*, who modeled God's love within and for the domestic Church; *Saints for Communities*, who served Jesus through various roles and professions; and *Saints for Sacraments*, who showed great love for the sacraments.

The eight books in *Saints of the Beatitudes* (a word meaning "a list of blessings from God") introduce nine holy people who exemplify attributes Jesus articulated in his Sermon on the Mount. Faustina Kowalska's diary, *Divine Mercy in My Soul,* read by millions, helped spread God's message of mercy. Patrick, a missionary, brought Christianity to Ireland. Monica prayed her wayward son, Augustine, would return to the faith. He did and was canonized. Katharine Drexel abandoned her comfortable life to become a nun. Carlo Acutis shared his faith and love of the Eucharist through technology. Bernadette Soubirous experienced visions of the Blessed Virgin Mary. Pope John XXIII convoked the Second Vatican Council, hoping to revive the Church. Jude was an apostle of our Lord.

Which saint was captured by pirates and sold into slavery? Name the saints with back-to-back feast days (August 27–28). Who gave $20 million to build churches and schools? Who created a website about eucharistic miracles? Who did Jesus appear and speak to? Who said, "My job is to inform, not to convince"? Who wrote *Peace on Earth* in 1963? Who is the patron of impossible causes? Find out in the *Saints of the Beatitudes* set—part of the *Saints and Me!* series—and help children connect to the lives of the saints.

Introduce your children or students to *Saints and Me!* as they:

—**READ** about the lives of the saints and are inspired by their stories.

—**PRAY** to the saints for their intercession.

—**CELEBRATE** the saints and relate them to their lives.

Free activities for children to use with this book may be downloaded at Liguori.org.

The Beatitudes

Divine blessings Jesus names in his Sermon on the Mount

Matthew 5:3–12

Saints of the Beatitudes

Patrick

Blessed Are the Poor in Spirit (Verse 3)

Monica and Augustine

Blessed Are the Mournful (Verse 4)

Katharine Drexel

Blessed Are the Meek (Verse 5)

Carlo Acutis

Blessed Are the Righteous (Verse 6)

Faustina Kowalska

Blessed Are the Merciful (Verse 7)

Bernadette

Blessed Are the Pure of Heart (Verse 8)

Pope John XXIII

Blessed Are the Peacemakers (Verse 9)

Jude the Apostle

Blessed Are the Persecuted (Verses 10–12)

Saint Katharine Drexel loved Jesus very much. She was meek and humble, just like Jesus. She treated people with love and respect, especially the helpless and the poor. In 1891, she started a religious order of missionary sisters who would teach in schools for Native and Black Americans.

Katharine was born in Philadelphia, Pennsylvania, in 1858. Her father was a successful banker and one of the richest men in America. The Drexels taught their children to be kind and generous to others. They gave a lot of money to charities (places that help people in need). "We are a very lucky family. We should share what we have with others," said her father.

Katharine and her sisters, Elizabeth and Louise, grew up in a loving and faith-filled home. Daily prayer and going to Mass helped their family grow closer to God. Several times a week, Katharine's mother gave food, clothing, and money to the poor in the city. The girls were always ready to help!

During the warm summer months, the Drexels stayed at their home in the country. It was a large home surrounded by tall trees and grassy meadows. The girls loved riding their horses, playing in the gardens, and taking long walks in the countryside with their parents.

Their family took exciting vacations all over the United States and Europe. During a trip to the western part of the United States, Katharine saw poor areas where Native Americans lived. She did not like what she saw. *"I have so much, and they have so little. Maybe someday I will be able to help them,"* she thought to herself.

Years later, their mother became very ill. Katharine, then in her twenties, took care of her until she died. During this sad time, Katharine turned to God in prayer. While praying for her mother, she felt God calling her to become a nun. "God, show me how to serve you," she whispered.

Sadly, two years later, their father died. Elizabeth, Katharine, and Louise were heartbroken. The sisters talked about what to do with the large amount of money their father had left them. "Father always taught us to share what we have with others," Katharine said. So they gave money to Native American missions, missionaries, and their father's favorite charities.

Katharine wanted to do more to help people, but she needed time to think and pray. “Let’s take a trip to Europe,” Elizabeth suggested. “That is a great idea,” said Katharine. Soon the three sisters were on their way to Europe!

While in Rome, Katharine met with Pope Leo XIII. "Holy Father, please send missionaries to the United States," she begged. "The Native Americans are very poor and no one will help them." The wise Pope smiled at Katharine and said, "My dear child, I think you would be a very good missionary. God is calling you to help others." Katharine was shocked! She thanked the Pope and hurried out the door. Now she was so confused she didn't know what to do.

On her trip home to Philadelphia, she thought about what the Pope had said to her, "God is calling you." She prayed a lot. Katharine asked her spiritual director, Bishop James O'Connor, for advice. He said she should join the Sisters of Mercy. "They will teach you everything you need to know."

When Katharine entered the convent, she surprised the whole world! Why would a very rich young woman give up everything to become a sister? Her answer was simple. She loved God and wanted to help poor and forgotten people, Native, and Black Americans.

After two years with the Sisters of Mercy, Katharine started her own order of missionary sisters. The sisters traveled to the west and southwest United States to begin their work. "We will teach about the Catholic faith, especially love for Jesus Christ in the Eucharist," she said. They were called the Sisters of the Blessed Sacrament. Katharine was now called Mother Katharine.

"All people have the right to a good education," she told her sisters, "and they should be treated like everyone else!"

Mother Katharine used her family's money to pay for many projects. She built schools, missions, and convents. She visited each one to make sure they had good teachers and the supplies they needed.

Her work was not easy. Sometimes people did not like what she was doing. "Why do you care about poor people? You should forget about all of them," they said angrily. Mother Katharine stared at them and said, "Oh, I am sorry, but you are wrong. God made all people, and we should treat people with kindness and respect."

Some mean people tried to stop her from doing her good work. But she was not afraid! She continued to build schools and missions across the country. Mother Katharine trusted God and prayed for his guidance. Sometimes people's hearts were changed because they knew she was doing the right thing.

At age seventy-seven, Mother Katherine became very ill. Doctors told her, "You must slow down and rest." For the next twenty years, she spent her life in quiet prayer. She prayed for her Sisters and for people who were unfairly treated.

After her death, the Sisters of the Blessed Sacrament continued working to make life better for Native and Black Americans.

Saint Katharine Drexel is remembered for her love of the Eucharist, service to the poor and generous spirit. Canonized by Pope Saint John Paul II in 2000, she is the second American-born saint, following Saint Elizabeth Ann Seton.

What can you do or what will you share
To show someone you really care?

♥ ♥ ♥

Saint Katharine Drexel,
You loved Jesus Christ in the Eucharist,
And he gave you the strength to do his work.
Give me a heart for the poor and helpless,
So that I also may do God's work. Amen.

GLOSSARY (NEW WORDS)

Charity: A group that gives money or goods to help people in need

Convent: A house where a group of women religious live

Generous: Sharing or giving more than what is expected, being unselfish

Heartbroken: A feeling of great sadness

Meek: Gentle, humble; being patient when you are unfairly treated

Mission: A community of people who live and work together; missions are served by religious leaders who start schools and churches and preach the gospel

Missionary: A person who teaches the faith or preaches the gospel in a certain place

Mother: The superior or leader of a group of women religious

Native Americans: Tribal groups of people native to the United States

Sisters of the Blessed Sacrament: A group of women religious started by Saint Katharine Drexel in 1891

Sisters of Mercy: A group of women religious started by Catherine McAuley in 1831

Spiritual Director: One who guides people in their faith

One of Saint Katharine Drexel's greatest achievements was the founding of Xavier University in New Orleans, the first Catholic university for Black students.